50 Ways to Be a Better Teacher

Professional Development Techniques

Chris Mares

WAYZGOOSE PRESS

Fifty Ways to Be a Better Teacher-
Professional Development Techniques
Copyright © 2015 by Chris Mares

ISBN-10: 1-938757-21-1
ISBN-13: 978-1-938757-21-1

Book design by DJ Rogers.
Edited by Dorothy Zemach.
Published in the United States by Wayzgoose Press.

Table of Contents

Teaching Techniques

1. Always Answer Questions

Students ask teachers questions for different reasons – the most obvious being that they want or need
to know the answer to a particular question. Other
times, they ask simply because they feel that it's a
way of being heard or recognized. Finally, some students will ask teachers questions to either show off
their own knowledge or challenge that of the teacher.

As teachers, we must answer our students' questions,
provided they are appropriate and relevant. However,
we don't have to answer them immediately, especially
if we are unsure of how to answer or unsure whether
our answer is, in fact, correct.

If you're unsure of an answer or don't know the answer
to a particular question, don't brush it off or make excuses. Rather, note the question down and tell the student or class that you will find the answer and get back
to them. Give the student positive feedback for asking
an interesting or challenging question. Of course, it is
essential to follow through: find the answer and make
sure that you get back to the student and give them
a satisfactory answer. If you think the question was
one from which the whole class would benefit, then
build in time to acknowledge the student, address the
question, and finish by encouraging students to ask
questions.

To make up an answer or to give a babbling explana-
tion does no one any good, especially the teacher. If
you are ruffled or rattled, this will be apparent to your
students, who will lose confidence in your abilities and

also lose trust in your judgment. On the other hand, to admit you don't know an answer is honest. Stating that you don't know the answer but you know where to find the answer, and then following through, will earn you trust and respect. Teachers need to be honest, consistent, and reliable.

Inevitably, students will ask some tricky grammar questions. A preemptive strategy is to arm yourself with a good grammar book for teachers or an English usage book, or bookmark some websites that serve the same function. For me, Michael Swan's *Practical English Usage* (Oxford University Press) was a useful go-to book. The explanations are simple and the examples are authentic.

Having the resources is one step; another is to browse the resources in advance. Think about questions that could come up in a certain lesson, such as why we use direct or indirect speech or when we use the past perfect. That way, you can brush up in advance if necessary.

A final point is that it is important to develop a positive attitude to student questions, not a defensive one. To welcome questions shows students that you are interested not only in your subject but also in them. Answering questions authentically and honestly will increase students' respect and also improve your self-confidence and skills at giving explanations.

2. Delegate

There are many ways to get students engaged in the process of learning. One is to delegate. For example, I am not very adept with technology. It is not intuitive to me, and I bumble. Of course there are many students with technological skills, some of whom may be motivated students and some of whom won't be. Asking a student who is not so motivated to assist with technology may validate that student in a way that empowers and motivates them. This can be done as a one-off or in a more formalized manner. Deploy technical assistants (TAs) for the day or the week. Entrust them with setting up computers, projectors, or sound systems. Or simply give a student the volume control. The teacher is the director of the class, but that doesn't mean the teacher has to have responsibility for everything.

TAs are useful for teachers. The role of a TA is a validating and inspiring one for the students themselves. There are different ways that roles can be attributed. Students can be designated, they can volunteer, or there can be a rotating roster. Here are some other areas where students can be given responsibility: recording attendance, collecting homework, giving out materials, organizing supplies, handling equipment, taking roll.

TAs can be Technical Assistants; they can also be Teaching Assistants. A Teaching Assistant can help model activities with the teacher. Rather than call on a number of students throughout a class, a teacher can choose one student to be the Teaching Assistant for the class or for a portion of the class. Again, this is an opportunity to work on student buy-in and engagement. Just make sure that every student has the chance to be a TA over the course of your term.

Of course, not all of these possibilities will work with all classes, given the varieties of levels, class size, and teaching context we face. Nevertheless, there is always something that can be tried.

The bottom line is that delegating works for both the teacher and student, as long as it is done in a principled and equitable way. Giving a responsibility to a reluctant or disengaged student may work to motivate them or it may not. Nevertheless, it is worth trying. If a student is resistant, then gently encourage – but don't push or make someone feel guilty or inadequate for not wishing to assume a responsibility.

If we model appreciation and gratitude, and are accepting of student mistakes or lack of knowledge, then we can establish an atmosphere of mutual respect and trust.

3. Don't Over-Prepare

Preparation is a vital aspect of any teacher's craft. However, over-preparation is time consuming and exhausting. Over-preparation can mean different things; for example, spending too much time searching for material or spending too much time creating material.

The process of preparation is straightforward. It should be driven by SLOs (student learning outcomes); that is, what you want students to learn, be able to do, or to have done by the end of class. The bottom line is that the class must have an outcome. The preparation involves providing the material or activities to achieve that outcome. Ask yourself: Are the materials or activities interesting, engaging, and appropriate to student needs and interests? If the material comes from a required text, ask: How do I make this chapter or unit interesting and engaging for students?

Teaching is about choice. Choose materials and activities that you feel meet the above criteria and commit to them. Work with what you've got. Don't continue to search for what you think might be better materials. Teacher energy is better spent thinking about how best to maximize the materials or activities you have chosen.

4. Echo

Echoing is an efficient and non-judgmental technique for correction of oral mistakes. For example, consider the follow exchange:

> **T:** What did you do on the weekend?
> **S:** I go shopping.
> **T:** You went shopping?
> **S:** Yes. I went shopping.

The student has made a simple error, and the teacher echoes the preferred response in question form. The student hears the question, becomes aware of the error, and repeats the preferred form.

This technique needs practice and should be used judiciously. It shouldn't be used for every error, only those that either interfere with communication or forms that the teacher is working on with a specific class or student. The teacher's voice should be clear, but not so loud as to stop the flow of student speech. If the student does not self-correct, the teacher must decide whether to let the error go or to continue to echo, or perhaps to draw attention to the error in another way.

It is useful to also note down errors either as they are made or at the end of class, in order to address matters such as verb tense or word form in a more formal way at another time.

5. Recycle

Part of the teacher's job is to help students understand new language, but an equally important job is to help them move language from their short-term memory to their long-term memory. A vocabulary test at the end of the week serves no useful purpose unless the items tested are continually recycled over time, so that students see them in similar but different environments.

Recycling is not the same as repetition. The trick is to visit items in slightly different contexts. Teachers need to keep a running list of new high-frequency items or structures and look for opportunities to use them in the classroom. Encourage students to record new items and to write example sentences with target words. Rather than always writing sentences using new words, students should also be encouraged to return to earlier words and recycle those.

On a simple level, questions such as, *What are you doing this weekend?* or *What did you do last weekend?* give students a reason to recycle common words and phrases. One especially effective way to recycle is to read on a regular basis and make a conscious effort to look for and make note of target language.

Repetition is important; but recycling is more important and should be an aspect of all principled teaching.

6. Rehearse

I do a lot of one-week teacher training workshops. At the end of the week, after modeling activities, having students observe classes, and much reflection and discussion, I have trainees prepare mini-lessons for Friday's teaching practice. On Thursday I tell trainees to think about what they will actually say to their students, rather than what they will have them do. For example, if the first step in an activity after schema-raising is to get students into pairs, what do you say? Do you say, *Get into pairs, Work with a partner,* or something else? Do you support your command with a gesture, or show how one pair will turn to face each other?

This is what I mean by rehearsal. It gives the teacher a chance to practice giving clear and concise instructions. We often plan lessons and think to ourselves, *First I'll have them talk about a trip they enjoyed,* but we don't necessarily consider the actual words we will say to our students. We need to. Clarity of instructions is crucial.

It is particularly important at lower levels where clarity is vital, especially if you are managing a larger class. Write down the actual instructions. Make notes about what you will model, and how. Rehearse. Do this by standing up and saying the instructions out loud just as you would to the class you will be teaching. This will give you a chance to check if your instructions are clear enough and also if they are pitched at the right level.

7. Remember Names

It's important to develop an ability to remember names. To know a student's name and to use it is to validate them. It is respectful and gives students a sense of self-worth. It also shows you care about your students and your teaching. If you care, your students will invest themselves in your classes.

It can take some time and organization, however, especially if your students have names that you are not familiar with. There are some basic techniques worth experimenting with, such as seating charts and the use of name badges or folded name cards on the desk. With smaller classes, a game of "Find Someone Who..." in the first class will give you time to monitor the class and familiarize yourself with students' names.

By the same token, we need to tell our learners how we expect to be addressed. In my case, I ask to be called *Chris*, and not *Mr. Chris* or *teacher*. It is also important to take into account the culture of the institution where you work. If all teachers go by first names, then go by your first name. By the same token, if everyone is called by their family name – for example, *Mr. Mares* or *Professor Mares* – then do the same.

Even if it takes a few classes for you to finally remember all the students' names, the effort will be appreciated.

8. Speak Clearly

Speaking clearly is a requirement for good teaching. If a teacher doesn't speak clearly and with authority, it's difficult for students to understand and remain engaged.

Nervous speakers tend to mumble, look down, and speak too quickly. They are more likely to backtrack and comment out loud on their own speech. For example, a teacher may begin giving an instruction and then say, *No, actually, let's not do it like that, let's try something different. OK?* For lower-level students, this type of self-commentary can be very confusing.

Beginning teachers can tend to rush their speech, as they don't want to be the center of attention. They'd rather be working with individual pairs or small groups because this is less intimidating. However, if the initial instruction to the class as a whole has been unclear, then all subsequent interactions with students are a form of damage control.

To be effective, new teachers may have to develop a modified voice delivery, one that is stronger and more authoritative than their usual speech. It may have to be more modulated and more intentional in tone, though not patronizing or unnecessarily deliberative.

However, the positive washback effect will be immediate and will lead to an increase in confidence.

9. Teach All Students

Beginning teachers often respond primarily to the enthusiastic and responsive students. Teachers gravitate towards these students because they make the teacher feel better about what he or she is doing. They ground the class in what the teacher believes is a successful narrative – the 'good class.'

True teaching, however, requires that we reach the students at the edges, the ones who might slip by the wayside. The marginal. The late student. The sleeper. The furtive phone checker. These are the ones we must bring in. Welcome. Forgive. And embrace.

For a new teacher, it is hard to risk a public interaction with a reticent student. What happens if they don't respond? What happens if they say something inappropriate? What happens if they don't understand what you are saying? The thought of awkward situations like this can be very unsettling.

The first step to teaching all students is to commit to an inclusive class and then pledge that you will find a way to reach everyone. One step at a time.

The reflective teacher should continually be considering their own class: *Why is it that I always let the 'better' students answer? What is it that's stopping me from asking all students? What is it that makes me uncomfortable when a student doesn't answer or resists me?* These are the valuable, deep structure questions that will lead to inclusive teaching.

10. Teach Responsively

It has been said that students learn despite what we do. Of course this should not be understood as permission for us to do anything we like, regardless of our students' responses. Our primary goal is to design our teaching around our students' needs and interests and to teach purposefully and efficiently.

To do this we must also teach responsively; that is to say, we must be sensitive to how students are reacting to activities or materials. If necessary, we should make on-the-spot modifications or sometimes change direction completely. This entails a willingness to depart from lesson plans when and where necessary. This requires us to constantly monitor students' level of interest in our classes, whether the material is too easy or too demanding, and whether all students are engaged. We should also be prepared to seize teaching moments when they occur.

Our teaching should not be a matter of making students 'do' what we have decided they should do. We should be sensitive, flexible, intentional, and deliberative. To teach responsively means that teachers and students are working together. Finding this balance requires careful and sensitive monitoring and a degree of flexibility.

11. Think on Your Feet

We encourage our students to operate at the edge of their ability spectrums, not from deep in the safety zone. This approach is principled, and we need to apply it to ourselves.

To think on one's feet means to improvise, to move away from the script, and to stand on stage in front of students and make principled choices that result in effective and efficient learning.

Many of us plan thoroughly and stick to our plans. At the same time, we realize, on reflection, that we could and should have done things differently. This sense of realization marks the start of the process of learning to think on your feet.

If you find it difficult to be spontaneous, begin to look for moments when you could have taken a lesson in a different direction. Begin a log and record these possibilities. As time passes, think about what you would have done and how you would have proceeded down that path before coming back to your original plan.

Next, take one of these moments when it comes around again and see what happens. There doesn't need to be a perceived outcome other than the fact that the 'moment' provided a useful opportunity for you to do something relevant, interesting, and engaging, that wasn't on your original plan. Record what you did and why, and what happened. Note how you got back to the original lesson plan or how you wrapped up the 'moment' you took.

Think of thinking on your feet as a form of awareness, an attempt to both monitor what you are doing and be sensitive to possibility.

12. Use Schema Raising

The best teaching occurs when students are engaged and interested. Starting a class by saying, *Today we're going to look at Unit 6*, or *Today we will look at processes* will fail to interest or engage most students.

Imagine I am going to teach a class on processes using total physical response (TPR), and the activity demonstrates how to make a pot of tea. To engage the students I could ask, *Do you know what I drink in the morning with my breakfast?* I then elicit responses and have students ask each other. I could ask, *What do you think your friends drink in the morning? How about your parents?* There are all sorts of possibilities. I could then ask how many people like tea; then how many people know how to make a pot of tea. At this point, I ask, *How many people would like to know how to make a real pot of English tea?* We brainstorm what we need and the verbs required, and I then have students stand up and make tea, using visualization techniques: *You are in the kitchen, turn on the faucet and fill your kettle with water*, etc.

Schema raising is artful and takes time to perfect, but it's central to efficient teaching. Think of it as performance. Think storytellers or stand-up comedians. Through schema raising, we generate the interest and energy we need for effective teaching. It's a wonderful feeling to sense one's students leaning forward in anticipation of what you're going to say or do. At that point, they are yours.

13. Use Effective Discipline

Rather than thinking of discipline as punishment, think of it as an aspect of classroom management and a requirement for effective teaching.

Brainstorm a list of behaviors you expect and behaviors you will not accept. For those behaviors you are not prepared to accept, make a note of what action you will take if you encounter this behavior. Next, edit the list and put it into language that you know your students will be able to understand.

If you start of with an unclear discipline plan and do not immediately respond to disruptions, it will be hard to manage the class. Conversely, when expectations are clear and you follow through with consequences, classroom management will be much easier.

Deal with any disruption immediately and with as little interruption as possible.

Make it clear that disciplining is nothing personal, and that it is directed against behaviors that take away from effective use of classroom time. Never humiliate a student in front of the class. If you need to talk with a student about their behavior, do it in private. Be clear, authoritative, consistent, and fair, and as free of emotion as possible.

The key to effective discipline is consistency in maintaining high standards of behavior. Be positive, creative, organized, flexible, enthusiastic, welcoming, and have a sense of humor.

14. Expand Your Repertoire

All teachers have materials and activities they prefer over others. We also have the tendency to stay with what we know and depend on the familiar. This is natural, but it can lead to stultification. We get into patterns and routines, and what may have once seemed interesting and engaging to students can lose its allure.

For this reason, we should always be on the lookout for new ideas. We need to experiment, particularly in areas that we don't tend to gravitate to. For example, a teacher may do a lot of work with writing and grammar but not pay much attention to pronunciation. This, I would argue, is therefore an area that this particular teacher needs to work on. I might suggest *Jazz Chants* (Carolyn Graham; Oxford University Press) especially if the teacher is either not used to or not comfortable with leading group chants. This may sound counter-intuitive, but it's not. Expanding our repertoire means growing in the areas we are not familiar or comfortable with, not simply adding on to areas where we already feel comfortable.

With the Internet, it's easy to search out new activities or skill areas. To add to our repertoire in a meaningful way, we need to be systematic, organized, and intentional. Set a goal of finding one new activity a week and trying it. If it doesn't prove successful the first time, critique yourself and try again. We need to not only add to our repertoires but to become adept at using the materials, activities, or techniques we add.

Readers of this ebook can email the publisher, Wayzgoose Press, at editor@wayzgoosepress.com to request one free teaching tips ebook (see the available titles, in areas such as pronunciation, grammar, speaking, writing, technology, teenagers, young learners and more, at: http://wayzgoosepress.com/education.html).

Personal Development

15. Have a Book in Your Pocket

I was once a reader for the blind English poet and critic James Reeves. It was a rare and wonderful experience. After school, I would walk through the sleepy streets and twittens to James' house, where I would read the *Times* editorials, his correspondence, and any proofs or poems he was working on. I was in the presence of a master. James was a crafter of words and an appreciator of good writing. When I told James I wanted to write, he told me to always carry a book in my pocket. There are so many moments in a day, he told me, when you could be reading – at a bus stop, between classes, on a walk, anywhere.

I took his advice. At first I would carry slim novels with me, then poetry, and after a while, I always kept a novel and an anthology of poetry in my bag.

It was the anthology of poetry that taught me the value not only of reading, but more particularly, rereading. I began to realize that the love of a poem could become a lifelong relationship. This became true of Walt Whitman's "Leaves of Grass," a poem that I can dive into anywhere and feel the beauty of Whitman's world with its democracy of observation and the significance he gives all things.

I discovered, through this practice, that simply reading a familiar line or stanza could be enough to change how you feel or think at a particular moment. A Shakespeare sonnet, for example, or a Billy Collins poem can lighten your heart or put a reflective smile on your face. You can be transported from the worries of the present to a more reflective and philosophical place.

This all began a long time ago, but it's a practice I maintain to this day. When waiting for students to arrive, I read. It's not only a pleasurable physical experience; a book requires a focus that an iPhone does not. Reading for pleasure is not a frenetic activity. It calms and stills your being. Turning a page slowly is a meditative practice and a tactile experience.

Being seen to be a reader says a lot about who you are and what you value. As teachers, we influence those we teach in many ways. And as teachers, we have a responsibility to model practices we value not only for ourselves but for others, too.

As a teenager, I used to deliver newspapers in the small village where I grew up. One of my weekend pleasures was to walk the mile and a half into the little Sussex town of Lewes and treat myself to a book. I remember the time I walked in to the bookshop one gray November morning, looked at the Picador collection, and bought *The Cement Garden*, by Ian McEwan. It was a book I carried in my pocket, and one that changed my life – it revealed a world that I found familiar and yet hadn't been taught about. I realized that books had the power to educate me and show me things in a way that my parents and teachers couldn't.

16. Find a Mentor

I think of the term *mentor* in different ways. The first is as someone we can seek out to advise us, and one who will also observe and instruct us. This two-way street is important. For me, the second aspect is the more important. In my experience, it is rare for teachers to voice their weaknesses or vulnerabilities. Teaching, although a public endeavor, is also intensely private: once the door to a classroom is closed, each teacher is on their own, free to succeed and fail in isolation. By extension, they are also free to report on what they do as they wish. Being human, we dwell on perceived successes and the 'good' classes, and we don't always have an accurate record of what we do or how we do it.

This is where a mentor can help. Successful mentoring depends on various factors. A mentor must be an experienced teacher, and a wise and reflective teacher also. They must be empathetic, sympathetic, and committed to helping colleagues grow as unique professionals in their own right, not simply as clones. These teachers exist, and they should be actively sought out. The trust factor is pivotal. New teachers feel apprehensive and afraid of failure, and a mentor must create a channel of communication that allows for candid discourse. A teacher should be able to voice all fears or concerns to a mentor and expect positive and constructive feedback.

Many institutions have mentor systems in place. Some are well-organized and constructive. Others are simply nominal; that is to say, a senior teacher is assigned to mentor a new teacher but not much happens.

I suggest that teachers at any stage in their career seek out a mentor or even mentors. I have mentors who are fellow teachers – though not necessarily of English nor even of an academic subject. I have been lucky enough to have mentors whom I regard as elders. These are wise people, either retired or no longer shouldering the responsibilities they once had, who have experience and wisdom that can be passed on.

In the US, educators look to research and policy for guidance. We have lost the concept of the 'village' and the need to look to our elders for guidance. Research strives for evidence-based efficiency in a quantitative sense, and that of course is valuable too. But an elder provides guidance from experience and wisdom; that is to say, from a reflective and considered perspective.

Research tells you that we have multiple intelligences; wisdom tells you that students will learn despite what you do.

17. Listen and Take Notes

Keep a notebook handy at all times. Listen to what people actually say in their interactions. This will enhance your knowledge as a cultural and linguistic informant.

As a writer of listening scripts, I have always been fascinated by the tension between what people actually say and the need to present certain structures or lexical items/chunks. For example, when I first moved to the US from England, I often heard interactions such as:

A: What's up?
B: How's it going?

The scenario is a college campus and two students walking past each other in opposite directions. Interestingly, B doesn't respond to A's question but responds with a similar question that A fails to respond to. This authentic data I collected and diligently recorded in my notebook helped me understand that the exchanges, while grammatically questions, were functionally greetings – not information that I found in my textbooks for beginners.

I live in the US, so I am constantly able to monitor interactions between people. If you live and teach in a non-English speaking country, you may find yourself listening to the exchanges of ex-pats or non-native speaker colleagues interacting in English. You can also listen to spoken interactions on the Internet as well as television, movies, radio, and podcasts.

Language is evolving. It is also regional. I teach students from around the world who have come to the University of Maine to further their educational aspirations. Many of them, after a few months, find themselves interacting with, or at least exposed to, locals speaking. Naturally, motivated and perceptive students will pick up on local variations. For example, this winter I heard an Iraqi student telling a fellow teacher that it was "wicked cold outside"; *wicked* being a regional substitute for *extremely* (or, in some contexts, a synonym for *awesome*).

This is an example of a student monitoring language. It is important for teachers to do the same. Language sensitivity, in terms of usage, means we can model and present language more authentically to our learners.

As a materials writer and teacher, I have often reflected on the language presented in coursebooks. I ask myself whether a native speaker would ever use the utterances that are presented, especially as listening materials. For example, I have never been asked, *Do you have any hobbies?* by a native speaker. I have, on the other hand, had my students ask each other this kind of question.

Notebook in pocket, it is very informative to listen to small talk to see what people actually *do* say.

18. Meditate

The mind is a busy place, and it's easy to lose one-self in the stress of busy days. This can be particu-larly true for teachers with demanding schedules and heavy teaching loads. Naturally, when the mind is constantly busy, and experiencing stress and anxiety, we become tired, run down, and sometimes depressed. However, when caught in the throes of frenetic lives, it's not always apparent that this is happening. It makes sense, then, to be proactive and take action to ensure that a situation like this doesn't occur.

There are, of course, many different answers; but one practice that will certainly provide benefits is medita-tion.

Like exercise regimens, there are many different forms of meditation, and many are aspects of vari-ous reflective practices, some religious and some not. From my perspective the goal of meditation is to sep-arate oneself from the stresses and distractions of the present, such as the classes that need to be prepared for or papers that need grading. As such, meditation is a way of learning to see what is *really* going on, rather than being consumed by what is *apparently* going on. Nothing changes, only our relationship to what is. In this sense, meditation is a form of realization and a change in the way we connect to our thinking.

Regardless of the form of meditation, the goal is the same – a clearer mind, one that is less distracted by the trivial and better able to see the bigger picture. The results of meditation are clear: lower blood pressure, less stress, better ability to rest, and more energy. We also hope for a better understanding of ourselves and what truly matters.

I have found certain forms of exercise to be meditative, especially running. However, cycling, swimming, cross-country skiing, and paddling have had the same effect. For physical exertion to be meditative, there needs to be a repeated and regular action over time, one which becomes automatic. At the point where the action becomes something that occurs without thought, a form of dynamic meditation occurs. Any runner will know the feeling of being 'in the zone,' where one's whole body is working as one with a steady breathing pattern. It's at that point we can let go. Running has the additional benefit of releasing endorphins, which create the aptly named 'runner's high.'

Success depends on making the time to practice on a regular basis and sticking with it. At first, the development of a new routine or habit can be difficult, particularly if you're not in the mood. It's important to remember that the time to really do it is when you are not in the mood or too tired. I know this from the many times I went running even though all I wanted to do was sit on the couch and drink a cup of tea.

And, as with many other new activities or interests, it's important to not overdo it. Better to do something three times a week for 20 minutes than aim for more and fail to reach your target.

19. Be Observed and Observe

One of the joys of teaching is the closing of the door to the classroom and the sense of autonomy that comes with it. There is a sense of possession, of control, and at the same time there is the potential for vulnerability.

Sometimes, though, that door will open, and an observer will enter, either scheduled, or unscheduled. Perhaps it's part of a review or reappointment process. Perhaps a student has complained. Or perhaps it is standard practice for a Director of Studies to observe teachers in action.

For many teachers, the presence of an observer in the classroom is stressful. If a teacher knows in advance they're going to be observed, they will often spend a great deal of time both preparing for the class and worrying about it. These reactions are counterproductive for different reasons. The first leads to over-preparing and a focus on putting on a show, while the second causes stress and anxiety. The latter will detract from the ability to teach spontaneously and to think on one's feet. In short, it will hinder a teacher's ability to teach.

Counter this type of situation by inviting selected teachers to observe your teaching and then offer feedback. At the same time, ask if you can observe one of your peers. Do this with someone you feel comfortable with and trust, such as a peer. Exchanging observations with a peer will probably be less nerve-wracking than being observed by a superior as a form of evaluation. You'll find too that the more you're observed, the easier it gets and the more comfortable you'll feel.

Approach observing from the perspective of information gathering, or looking for new ideas and techniques. What do other teachers do that you don't? How do they carry out the basic classroom functions such as giving instructions and feedback? How do the classes begin and end? What do they do with students who are not engaged, and with students who dominate the room? The more you observe, the more tools you will have available to you. At the same time, you can reflect upon your own skillset and begin to validate yourself and mark areas for growth.

In my teacher training, I emphasize the need to become comfortable with being uncomfortable. This is how growth and development occur. I used to find it very difficult to be observed when I was in training. Now, though, I feel at ease. I don't try to be someone I'm not. I have people observe me being me, the teacher I am.

20. Give Presentations

I encourage new teachers to think about submitting proposals for conferences at the local, regional, national, and international level. The process of reading through a request for proposals, followed by the writing process, from brainstorming to final draft, helps teachers reflect on what they do, why they do it, and how they do it. This process is rigorous and demands a focus that we might not always give to our everyday planning. It makes us consider our work at a deeper and more principled level. As such, it helps to professionalize us.

Presenting also provides the opportunity to work with one or more colleagues on a collaborative project. This process provides insight into what others do, and again allows teachers to validate or question their own practices.

I have spoken to teachers after observing classes and pointed out that what they were doing was worthy of sharing at a conference, and I have often been surprised by the reaction of teachers who said that they didn't think others would be interested in what they were doing. But I think the contrary is true.

Teachers spend a lot of time in their own minds preparing lessons and organizing their teaching. These thoughts are very individual and involve different ways of organizing and presenting material. Sharing systems of organization, ways of sequencing materials, teaching techniques, and materials helps everyone not only reflect on their own practice but also invites other teachers to experiment and develop their own skillset.

If you have developed an efficient system and put in the time and effort to make it effective and principled, then it is worth sharing. It's important to stand before peers and say, "This is our teaching context, these are our principles, these are our desired student learner outcomes, this is our curriculum, this is our approach, and this is how we implement and coordinate what we do." For the observing peers, this it is an opportunity to reflect on their own practice and to either validate what is already being done or see possibilities for how things might be done differently. For presenters, it's a chance to reflect, distill, and articulate current practice and to also get feedback from peers.

Submitting proposals for conference or workshop presentations makes us become more invested in what we do and also what our peers do. When feedback only comes from the institution where we work, it can be limited. Feedback from external perspectives can provide new and sometimes better ways of doing what we do.

For those who have not presented before and wish to get started, it's not as daunting as one might think. Start by attending a local or regional conference to get a sense of what topics are of current concern. Consider the different length and format of sessions. Go to poster sessions. Attend plenary addresses. Become part of the culture. When submitting a proposal, read the proposal requirements very carefully and follow them to the letter. Conferences often have a theme, and what you submit in your proposal needs to connect and appeal to a reader going through many proposals to select the most interesting and relevant.

It's possible your proposal will be rejected. This happens to everyone, and you should not take it personally and dwell too long on the disappointment. Reflect on your proposal and see if there is anything that could have been different or more appealing. Resubmit or modify it at a later date.

The process of submitting a presentation proposal will cause you to reflect on your own practice and to ask yourself why you do what you do; and this is a good question.

21. Write

Many teachers teach writing, and many teach very well indeed; however, not all of these teachers write. Writing is a skill that can continually evolve and develop. It can be the work of a lifetime. It is through writing that we can produce our most rigorous thinking. We can also demonstrate our creativity and respect for the beauty of language. For these reasons alone, all writing teachers should write not only to hone their own skills but also to be able to empathize with the process their learners are going through. Students need to hear that their teachers are still learners and are still working on developing their own skills.

The more genres we write in, the better. We can write texts, emails, letters, poems, short stories, blog posts, Facebook comments, essays, and papers. Whatever we do will mark an engagement that both we and our students will benefit from.

Modeling practices for our students can be very powerful. Like many writers, I carry a notebook with me at all times. I write down snippets of conversation; notes to myself; ideas for stories; to do lists; the names of musicians, writers, movie directors; and recipes. I encourage my students to do the same, and some do.

In the end, though, my students know I'm a writer, that I'm passionate about writing, and I am interested in their writing and helping them to become better writers.

22. Read Professionally

This may seem obvious, but for busy teachers it is not always easy to stay current. However, it is not that difficult to develop a reading routine that will enable you to find out what is happening in the world of research questions, best practices, the use of technology in the classroom, and so on.

Teaching blogs, such as the International Teacher Development Institute (iTDi) blog, are great resources. The posts – by teachers, for teachers – are practical, honest, and to the point. Moreover, none of them take more than a few minutes to read and ponder over. The effect is to absorb the thoughts, experiences, and ideas of fellow teachers and thus find yourself inspired and re-energized. Scott Thornbury and Jeremy Harmer have excellent blogs, and so do many of the bloggers who post regularly at iTDi, such as Barbara Hoskins Sakamoto.

The key is to be disciplined. Read professionally on a regular basis for a period of time that you know is achievable. Commit yourself to making notes.

Through reading blogs and journals, I have become intimately connected to a global community of passionate teachers doing wonderful work in very different contexts. I've connected to new friends and reconnected with old friends. I began to write more myself, and appreciate that there are others thinking and writing about issues of great concern to myself.

23. Remember the Good Teachers

We've all experienced many different teachers, and they have all impacted us in one way or another. However, there are some who stand out because they made a difference in a positive way.

It is interesting to reflect on these teachers and to ask what it was about them or what they did or said that made a difference. Some were just good and nice people who made an effort to teach and to validate their students. Others were driven by a passion for their subject and a sincere desire to pass this love on to their students. Others saw something in us, a glimmer of potential or interest, perhaps, and they worked on it until the glimmer began to shine.

Still others said something that stuck. I have a clear memory of a history class on Tudor England. After one class, our teacher asked if there were any questions, and I raised my hand. The teacher called on me and I asked my question. He smiled, scratched his head, laughed, and then said, "That's a good question and I honestly don't know the answer, but it's an interesting avenue we should explore." The fact that our teacher, who had a passion for his subject and great interest, was prepared not only to say that he didn't know the answer to my question, but also that my question led us to an interesting avenue that 'we' should explore, both validated and inspired me. I was probably fourteen at the time, but this comment had a profound effect on me and was the reason that I went on to take history as an 'A' level subject and then continue to read history at university.

That anecdote illustrates how a teacher, maybe unwittingly, can shape a student's life. I don't know if our teacher could see the impact he had on me, and really it doesn't matter. What does matter was that his attitude to students, his passion, and his honesty were consistent. If he made a difference to me, he would make a difference to others.

Go back in your mind to your beginnings in formal education. I expect you'll find that at every step of the journey there were one or more teachers who made a difference. This is not the same as liking a teacher or enjoying their classes. Sometimes we might find ourselves impressed by someone's energy or their organizational skills, or their ability to remember everyone's name and to show an equal interest in all students.

As you reminisce, you'll find teachers who made a difference to you. Write down the traits they had or what it was about them that inspired you and made a difference. When you've finished, study the list. Check the traits, actions, or comments and see which ones you already have and which ones you'd like to work on developing.

Attitude

24. Have an Open Door Policy

Many teachers, especially newer teachers, often feel vulnerable and threatened by having observers in their classrooms. Moreover, when they are observed, they can become overly concerned with themselves and how they appear to the observer, rather than focusing on making the most productive use of their time working with students.

Over time, this situation may become more extreme, and teachers can become territorial and protective of their classrooms, resenting and resisting observers.

Of course, this shouldn't be the case; and fortunately it doesn't have to be.

One point I make during my teacher training sessions is that it helps to become comfortable with being uncomfortable. This involves letting go of the need to have control over everything or to be completely committed to only one way of doing things.

If you're uncomfortable being observed, either formally or informally, it's important to get to the core of your fear. What is it about the presence of another person in the room, who is not a student, that you find so disturbing or unsettling? Do you feel inadequate or worry that you might fail to do something or make some glaring gaffe? Remember: the worst that can happen is probably a moment of embarrassment or an awkward silence, either of which can be easily dealt with by acknowledging it with acceptance and a smile.

Modeling our humanity is important. Sometimes things go wrong; that's part of life. Overall, the more you welcome others into your classroom, the more comfortable you will become.

25. Be a Champion

We must teach all students with equal conviction and find ways to inspire and engage the reluctant. I also believe in championing students; that is to say, investing effort in bringing on those students who are really struggling.

Reaching out to someone who seems to be teetering on the brink of failure or is simply not engaged can really turn a student around. We can't do this for all students all the time, but we can always do it for one particular student during a particular teaching session.

I had a recent experience with a student who seemed 'stuck.' He came to class often enough for him to think that he should be improving, but he didn't come enough or engage enough to actually improve. As a result, he became resentful and almost resistant. He was certainly dismissive of the classes he was in, saying that he already knew everything that was being taught and that he'd done it all before. He began pointing the finger at me, his other teachers, the teaching material, the curriculum, the tests, and the pedagogy we employ. He became obsessed with taking the TOEFL and demanded to take tests that were not appropriate for his level. The student became a topic of weekly faculty meetings and was seen as a nuisance and a disturbance.

This was a situation in which the student needed a champion. Clearly he was suffering. He felt isolated and misunderstood. He didn't feel his needs were being met or that anyone cared whether he succeeded or not.

This type of situation is not uncommon, especially for lower level students. We have all experienced it; and if we haven't, we will.

I met with the student and told him that I was worried because he seemed unhappy. He seemed surprised that I was focusing on his emotional state rather than his absences and tardiness. I asked him if he wanted to be happy again, and he said he did. We arranged to meet once a week for fifteen minutes in order to turn things around for him.

The time was spent creating an achievable and productive study plan. Rather than studying for six hours on Sunday, we agreed that one hour a day, every day, studying in a systematic fashion, would be enough.

We talked about study skills, active learning, student accountability, and the power that we all have to make a positive difference to ourselves. It wasn't easy to communicate this, but it was possible, one on one, over time.

The student began to be timely and attentive. He engaged and reaped the reward. He did it. Himself.

However, without taking the time to get the student refocused on himself and his own responsibilities, he might not have changed his attitude.

To champion a student takes time and effort, and also

a consistent plan. In the end, it is student motivation that will predict student success. But there are times when a student requires consistent individual attention and sincere interest in their success to rekindle the flame.

Championing a student fosters the development of empathy and negotiating skills. It helps us reflect on what is possible in the course of real time. To help a student realize that they have the power to change and also the responsibility for their own success is not always easy. The initial hurdle involves the student engaging in reflection and realizing that pointing the finger is non-productive, while asking high yield questions of oneself is productive.

We have to begin with bringing the student to the realization that the starting point is often, "What could I do differently?"

26. Be Consistent, Reliable... and Unpredictable

All students need their teachers to be consistent and reliable. This means starting and ending classes on time, teaching purposefully, maintaining a fair and equitable classroom, being there for all students, and having students demonstrate to both their teacher and themselves that they are learning. This is what being a professional and principled teacher means.

However, to keep students on their toes and to maintain their interest and engagement, it is necessary to have a degree of unpredictability. If, in the classroom, we always do the same things in the same way, there will inevitably come a time when what we do becomes routine and eventually monotonous.

There is a particular danger when teachers have to use a set curriculum or specific coursebook. The material may be interesting and suitable, but if every class begins with an instruction such as, *Today we're going to look at Unit 6* or *Open your books to page 49*, then the spark can be lost. The need to be unpredictable is dictated by the energy and engagement of the students. We must be constantly monitoring levels of interest and be keenly aware of when activities begin to flag.

To avoid this, we need to keep one step ahead and be unpredictable; we need to be able to switch things up. At times in the teaching year when things seem to be dragging, or students are stressed or unsinterested, take a part of the class or even the whole class to do something different. This could involve doing a new activity, watching something, having a guest teacher or speaker, going on a class trip, or anything else that would break the routine and serve to reinvigorate student interest.

Also, pay particular attention to schema raising. Find ways to develop curiosity and interest before starting an activity. There are many ways to be 'unpredictable' and yet principled from a pedagogic perspective. For example, in a writing class, inject some listening, reading, or conversation.

Keep a record of how frequently you do this. Build some time into your planning at the beginning of the term (or the month) to ensure that some flexibility is available for this to happen. Remember, there can be planned unpredictability; i.e., doing something new and unexpected that the teacher has prepared for, in addition to unplanned, spontaneous, unpredictability.

27. Make Your Classroom a Safe and Respectful Place

We know that students must make mistakes to learn and that taking risks is an important part of this process. However, we need to ensure that our students feel comfortable taking risks and are prepared to do so.

Many students are reluctant to take risks or make mistakes in front of their classmates. This is natural and understandable. It's our responsibility to make sure the atmosphere of our class is one in which students will feel comfortable and safe.

To do this, encourage effort and support students in their attempts to communicate. A student must never feel that they are struggling alone without help. Listen attentively, provide language where necessary, clarify if need be, and give students the time they need to feel that they have been listened to and acknowledged.

We also need to ensure that we respect all students and don't appear to have favorites. Furthermore, we need to communicate clear expectations of how students will interact with each other. Model the fact that we respect our students and that we expect our students to respect each other. It is not hard to do this, but it requires mindfulness and consistency.

For example, how you greet students as they enter the classroom makes a difference. You can test this yourself. If a student arrives late to class and you smile at them and usher them in, you will get a different response than if you frown or ignore them. For students to feel comfortable, they must feel welcomed and know that the teacher is on their side. Teachers have the power to be all-inclusive and to welcome all our students into the process of learning. This is something we must do – consciously.

28. Be Fair

I have been a trainee teacher, a new teacher, a developing teacher, and a teacher trainer, and throughout my experience I have observed a lot of classes in many different contexts. I have always found the act of observing to be fascinating and complex. To observe a single class out of context can only inform you of so much. It can tell you what the teacher did and what the students did in a particular class at a particular point in time, but it cannot reveal the process of teaching in a truly meaningful sense, which is to say – over time.

Nevertheless, through observation of new teachers, I have observed some patterns. A new teacher asks a question and a hand shoots up. The teacher, relieved by the response, calls on the student to answer. The next time the teacher asks a question, another student quickly responds. And so it continues, and the observer notes that responses, though good, are only coming from a certain number of students. The majority, in fact, are not responding. This may be something that the teacher doesn't actually notice, preferring simply to acknowledge that questions are being answered enthusiastically by engaged students. This may be enough for the teacher, who is also experiencing the stress of being observed.

Being fair to all students requires teachers to ensure that all students get their chance, and not simply in a nominal manner. Students are all different and need to be given their chances differently. Some students will respond immediately; others need time and need to know that a space is being kept for them by the teacher. Some students need teacher support, and others are more confident. Being fair means acknowledging the different needs of different students.

Being fair also means being available for all students in the ways they need. It also means managing the class in such a way that certain students do not dominate at the expense of others.

It is easy to see why teachers respond to eager enthusiasm, but we need to keep an eye out for all students. Be invested in all students learning, not just the most successful. The challenge is to engage and interest those who have not bought in until such time as they do. One of the pleasures of teaching is to turn around an unmotivated student or to see a reticent student begin to gain confidence and flower. This can only happen if we are fair.

Being fair is an ethical principle, but it also results in sound pedagogy. Moreover, it models a behavior that we want and then expect from our students. We must begin with the position that all students are equal – not in their abilities but in their right to become successful students, with the aid of their teacher and classmates.

29. Be Holistic and Humanistic

By this, I mean that we should not only be sensitive to each student in their individuality and entirety, but that we should also treat the class as a community that requires nurturing. In this way the teacher is an integral part of a shared experience, rather than simply a director of activities without concern for the individual students or the sense of community that is required for effective teaching and learning.

To me, being holistic and humanistic is fundamental to my beliefs not only as a teacher but as a learner and human being in a broader sense. We are social beings who value connectivity and meaningful association. Our identity in life comes from this, and through it we find life's meaning and purpose.

I also believe that this needs to occur in within a framework of compassion and peace. If we follow these beliefs, we will be focusing our teaching on our students as unique individuals, working with them at the place they are at any given point in time.

In order to teach like this, we have to believe, practice, and model these principles. Teaching this way takes conviction and effort, but the results, in my experience, are self-evident. Teaching with passion and compassion brings us closer to our students and our students closer to us. The concurrent development of trust and respect results in more engagement, more risk taking, more learning, and a more rewarding experience for students and teachers alike.

In many of the more traditional teaching contexts, the roles of teacher and learner are often oppositional. The holistic and humanistic model is one of unity and shared experience, in which everyone is respected and acknowledged as equally valuable and significant.

30. Be Interested

In my teacher training, I often tell trainees that low-level students may not understand what you say, but they will have an immediate visceral sense of *you*. They will tap into your energy and your enthusiasm – or your nervousness and trepidation.

A requirement of successful teaching is to be interested in teaching, and especially *interested in* your students. This is the first step to being *interesting to* your students. If as a teacher you are engaged, creative, responsive, flexible, reliable, and unpredictable, you will be interesting. Students engage with interesting teachers. They give back. Their affective filters lower, and they feel more comfortable taking risks and making the mistakes that are necessary for progress to be made.

On a practical note, it's is useful to jot down things that students tell you about – for example, the name of a book, poem, movie, or song. With the Internet, it's easy to check them out and get a sense of your students' tastes and interests. The next step is to follow up. If a student mentions a song they like, find it, listen to it, think about it, and then follow up with the student. Students appreciate it when their teachers remember things they've said. It's very motivating for a student to know that their teacher took time at home to listen to a song they find meaningful.

31. Be Yourself

Find your own inner teacher. Don't try to be someone else or to be like someone else. Tap into who you are, and begin there. Note what you're comfortable with and what you're not comfortable with. Build on your strengths and begin to work on any shortcomings, limitations, or inhibitions you may have. Learning to be an effective teacher and becoming the best teacher you can be takes time and effort. It's a journey, and one that's only truly meaningful if undertaken authentically as yourself.

A technique to help in this process of self-discovery is to step out of yourself and observe what you are doing in the classroom when you give instructions or interact with students. This requires a letting go of the emotions involved in teaching. Rather than responding emotionally when an activity appears not to be working, ask questions like, "How could I do this differently, so students are more engaged?"

Learning to be yourself – that is to say natural and at ease in the classroom – may not happen overnight, especially for new teachers or for teachers who like to keep a distance from their students.

This, to my mind, is one of the pleasures of teaching – the personal growth that occurs over time. Teaching is a complex art. There is a lot going on in every classroom at any particular time, and as teachers become more comfortable with the management of the class, they become more relaxed and comfortable and are able to emerge as more authentically themselves.

32. Cultivate Presence

As a student of Tae Kwon Do, I noticed that my master had a particular presence. He was a fifth dan black belt who had spent many years practicing his art and at the same time cultivating his one presence.

He had strength, ease, confidence, interest, control, and a generosity of spirit. His presence was both tangible and intangible. It was there when he spoke and there when he was silent. It existed in his physical presence: how he moved, how he breathed, and how he engaged with others.

Clearly my master had arrived; and yet, in his humility, he considered himself a student, still striving and still learning. There was something about his presence that was beautifully alive and inspirational.

Presence is something we can cultivate. It embodies our whole being, our mental state, our emotional state, and our physical state. It is who we are.

In order to develop presence, we need to think of teaching as a practice, like a martial art. There are physical aspects to teaching that need to be internalized through careful pacing and repetition: how we hold ourselves, how we breathe, how we make eye contact, how we smile and welcome others. These are all aspects of our presence. We need to reflect on what is stopping or blocking us, and work to remove these obstacles. This requires both reflection and honesty, as well as the desire to grow.

The presence we cultivate must be authentic and true to who are we are in our individual natures. There is no single model. We can easily be influenced by the brash confidence of a charismatic extrovert, but this is not necessarily the presence we would want to cultivate. The presence a teacher should strive for should result in trust and safety. Our students should feel that they will be respected and nurtured as individuals, and shown how to learn and grow.

The process is one of cultivation. It takes time and the development of practice. In the same way that my Tae Kwon Do master began as a white belt, so many new teachers must put in the hours of practice and repetition, and patiently wait for their confidence and skillset to expand and develop.

33. Establish Rapport

A teacher's relationship with a class takes time to develop. Create a good first impression by being organized, purposeful, interested, enthusiastic, confident, and friendly. Having made a good first impression, you can establish a rapport in much the same way. This occurs not just through how you present yourself, what you say, and how you act, but also by how you interact and show interest in your students. It should be noted here that I mean all students. Make eye contact with all students, address all students, show interest and concern for all students.

Learn student names quickly, and deal with discipline issues quickly and consistently without anger or sarcasm.

Be creative with your schema raising-activities and transitions. Be reliable but unpredictable.

Be culturally sensitive and show interest in your students' individual cultures, interests, and backgrounds. Welcome difference and diversity in terms of both practice and opinion.

Cultivate an atmosphere of trust by being open and respectful.

Share information about yourself, but not too much. Show that there are boundaries and that the boundaries matter.

34. Don't Be Like Them

It is easy to point to positive traits and behaviors that successful teachers exhibit. By the same token, we can also reflect on teachers who failed to engage us or displayed behaviors that were detrimental to an effective classroom.

My preference is to dwell on the positive and not to look to the negative. However, by occasionally doing so, it is easy to see the true value of the traits and behaviors we aspire to display.

If I let my mind return to my days at Lewes Comprehensive School, I can remember a number of teachers who struck me at the time as poor teachers. Students are sensitive and perceptive; they can immediately pick up on the energy a teacher exudes. If a teacher is disinterested, ill-prepared, tyrannical, unfair, inconsistent, humorless, sarcastic, bitter, or jaded, students will know immediately. Unfortunately, due to the power differential, it is possible for teachers to delude themselves and be in denial about what is happening in the class, and they can go through the motions of teaching without belief or commitment. Many times students will go along with the charade, as there is no obvious alternative. The result is the nominal classroom where both teacher and student follow their prescribed roles with nothing positive happening.

If a teacher has any of the above traits, then there will be a gulf between the teacher and the class that is unbridgeable. The class and teacher will be placed in an oppositional relationship, and this will have a tremendous impact on both teaching and learning.

The oppositional classroom does not result in efficient teaching or learning. Any negative trait or behavior can result in teachers and students being pitted against each other. As a result, we must look for ways to ensure that teacher and student are on the same side.

One way to ensure this is to be both rigorous and honest. In order to get the most out of our students, we must model the traits we wish them to have. In the end, what we invest of ourselves will come back to us. By the same token, what we fail to give will lead to a disconnect and dissatisfaction.

When I look back at the teachers who could have been better or could have done more, I see teachers who basically didn't want to be present. This is the lesson I take from these teachers – be present.

35. Remember That It's Not about You

This is a driving principle that I feel increasingly more strongly the longer I teach. Our guiding principle has to be the needs and interests of our students. We need to teach effectively and efficiently, with purpose and conviction. The center of our daily world needs to be our students; how we feel is secondary to our mission.

For example, if a student seems disengaged or is rude in any way, we need to not take this personally. We need to analyze the behavior from the student's perspective while asking ourselves whether we may have contributed to the situation through our own behavior or what we said. We should view situations through a positive and professional lens, and ask ourselves high-yield questions. If a student seems to be disengaged, perhaps they are simply having an off day, or they are tired, or they may feel they are not listened to or respected.

I know from years of observations that new teachers are emotionally vulnerable and are likely to take things students say or do personally. I think this is natural and so, early on, it's helpful to develop the ability to take a step out of yourself and move away from your personal emotional world and learn to see things with a purposeful and critical eye.

One strategy is to journal about incidents that occur in which you have taken something personally. Writing down what happened as dispassionately as possible enables the teacher to confront his or her vulnerabilities in a neutral space and to look at what happened more objectively. It also gives time for reflection.

36. Share

Sharing is a central aspect of healthy human relationships. Our closest friendships come through shared experiences. We share positive experiences and become closer; and we share hardships and become closer.

In the classroom, the teacher is often the 'knower,' the disseminator of information and knowledge, while the student is the learner. This power differential can create a tension in the teacher-student relationship and a gulf, separating them. In some teaching contexts, this can be culturally appropriate or pragmatically desirable. However, this distance creates an issue when we come to the matter of sharing.

Sharing, as an act, is one of giving, without the requirement of reciprocity. It puts the one sharing in a position of vulnerability, as their offer may be rejected.

I remember times when teachers shared experiences or anecdotes about their lives that made a difference to how I felt about them not only as teachers but also as people. Sharing can be a useful teaching tool, such as when students are experiencing something significant, or when there is a need to exemplify what is being taught or discussed. Moreover, the act of giving can foster both respect and interest.

Like all good things, sharing needs to be done judiciously. Information or anecdotes should be relevant and significant, and not incidental. The sharing must also be culturally and socially appropriate. Teachers do not need to (and should not) share all aspects of their lives. However, sharing something of yourself at an appropriate time will bring you closer to your class. It helps foster trust and respect, and as a modeling activity will give permission for students to do the same.

37. Take a Position

Being an effective English language teacher requires one to have a broad knowledge set and also principled beliefs on the role of the teacher and the learner. It also requires teachers to take a position on teaching the skills of listening, speaking, reading, and writing. Moreover, teachers need to consider how they will address grammar, vocabulary, pronunciation, as well as psychological, cultural, and interpersonal factors. They also need to consider the role of feedback and correction.

New teachers should know that it takes time to become the most effective teacher they can be. It takes time to get to know yourself as a teacher, to gain the confidence, skills, and experience that will enable you to work with students to the best of your ability.

Teachers also need to know that they may well change in both attitude and practice over time. I have seen teachers who have been committed to a particular pedagogy later abandon it in favor of another, as views on best practices changed.

Taking a position on the various aspects of teaching is vital, but the position needs to be taken in a principled way, and teachers need to be pragmatic rather than dogmatic. That is to say, they need to be open to new and different ways of doing what they do.

They need, in short, to be open to change.

Experimentation through trying different techniques or activities keeps you engaged and reflective. To always and only teach in one way becomes dull and routine. The automatizing of teaching so that it becomes rote and predictable can remove the spark of creativity and take the creative glint from the teacher's eye.

Take a stand, have sound reasons for doing what you do – but equally, be reflective and ask considered questions of yourself and your practice.

For example, a teacher may hold the belief that students need to memorize a certain number of words per day in order to become efficient language users. That is a position, but without more rigorous investigation, it is not a truly principled position. There are other questions that clearly need to be asked. For example:

- Which vocabulary items should be memorized?
- What is the principle of selection? According to perceived difficulty or frequency of usage, or something else?
- How should items be recorded? In translation? In English? With an example sentence? With synonyms and antonyms?
- How will items be recycled?
- How will students internalize these items over time, rather than simply consigning them briefly to their short-term memories?

Teachers need to approach their practice critically and reflectively. A position needs to be taken, but it should not be immutable. Teaching is a dynamic art. Fluidity and change keep it alive, whereas predictability and dull routine lead to a lack of engagement and motivation in teachers and students alike. Some of the most rewarding questions a teacher can ask are, *Why is it that I do what I do?*, *How could I do what I do differently to help motivate students?*, and most importantly, *What is it about me and what I do that most enables and most hinders my students?*

We know that learners learn despite what we do. The point is to make the process of learning as expeditious as possible. To do this, we need to have clear reasons for doing what we do, and a commitment to changing what we do if we discover better ways.

Physical Self

38. Exercise

There are obvious reasons for exercise in a general sense: it helps us control weight and fight various health conditions and diseases, it improves our mood, it increases our energy, it helps us rest more calmly, and it can be fun. These are all good reasons, but there are others that pertain to the teacher's life.

Building an exercise regimen means we are organizing and prioritizing things that matter. This has a trickle down effect into the rest of our lives, and helps us organize and prioritize in other areas.

Exercise is both cathartic and meditative. It relieves stress and creates the space for us to think and to reflect. On a personal level, many solutions to my problems and many of my best ideas have come when exercising.

Regular exercising is also modeling a behavior for students. It shows that you respect and value yourself, and that you do it partly so you can be a better teacher.

39. Look After Your Voice

Teaching is demanding, both physically and emotionally. Our minds can be so busy as we monitor, manage, and teach our students that sometimes we don't look after ourselves properly. One of our key teaching tools is our voice, and when we can overstretch our voice, it adds to stress and fatigue – and in the end, to less efficient teaching.

Here are some ways to take care of our voice. First, find time for a quiet period when you don't have to use your voice. Second, never talk above background noise if you don't have to. Wait for the noise to pass, or do something to make it not so audible, such as shutting a window or asking a neighboring teacher to lower the volume of a listening activity. If you need to attract your students' attention, don't shout. Use another technique such as clapping your hands, tapping on the board, or switching the light on and off.

Other basics include not spending too much time in cold dry air or sitting hunched over, which puts a strain on the neck muscles (check yourself now, as you're reading this book – are you sitting up straight?). Avoid irritating chemicals, such as those in commercial household cleaners. Overly spicy foods can also impact some people's voices. Finally, keep hydrated. Lubricate your throat. Carry water with you, and remember that caffeinated and carbonated beverages dry you out.

Your posture helps, too. Stand tall, with your shoulders back. Open your chest and keep your chin up.

This well help you project your voice with less effort and give you the confident bearing you need to use your voice effectively.

Finally, rest – not only your voice, but your body and mind, too.

40. Rest

Teaching can be very tiring. This is especially true for new teachers or teachers with new assignments. There are many reasons for this. Firstly, for new teachers, there is the anxiety and apprehension. We are all familiar with the questions that lurk in our minds such as, *Do I have enough material? Am I ready to teach? What if someone asks a difficult question? Will I be able to manage the class?* The process of reflection, which is an integral part of teaching, is something we can't turn off, and it continues outside the classroom and outside our working hours. This can also be tiring.

Apart from the pedagogical demands and constant human interactions that teaching requires, there are also the physical demands.

For these reasons, rest is vital. There is nothing quite like a good night's sleep to recharge a teacher and prepare them for another day. This has to be built into the professional routine. Teachers, like athletes, require stamina. They have to keep going. Not just for one class but for the teaching session, whether it's a term, semester, or other unit of time.

The simple fact is that adults need between seven to eight hours of sleep a night. Every night. There are health risks associated with sleep deprivation, and with enough sleep you feel better and can do more.

In addition to sleeping at night, it's important to rest periodically during the day, naps, downtime, and moments of solitude can all help. Teachers are busy people, but it's usually possible to find a few moments in a day when you can sit, alone, and close your eyes or put your head on the desk. A short walk by yourself can also recharge your batteries. Basically any quiet time without interruption can become a time of rest.

We know our students are tired by the end of the day. However, we sometimes forget how tired we are ourselves. We must also remember that fatigue is cumulative. If we don't get enough rest over time, we will lose our energy and our spark. We also become vulnerable to sickness.

For these reasons, we need to think of moments of rest and time to sleep as a requirement of teaching. We must schedule sleep and rest into our routine and make them habits that help us not only do the best we can, but also enable us to enjoy and continue the job we love.

41. Look Right

Students look for clues in a teacher's appearance and actions that will help them to form an impression of the teacher. Whether this impression is accurate or not, it will be a working hypothesis until new information leads to a change in the initial impression.

If you are from the same culture as a student, they will compare you to the expected norms for a teacher. If you are from another culture, you will be assessed in a more complex way, in terms of both the stereotype the student has for you and notions of what is appropriate within the culture where you're teaching.

Making an effort is important. Appearance is one area where students will viscerally respond to what they see. Remember, how you appear is a choice – and one that says things about you. For example, not really caring about how you dress may give students the impression you don't particularly care about other things, like your teaching or like them.

How we dress gives clear messages to our students. The message we want to give is that we care. We care about ourselves, we care about our position and responsibilities, we care about and respect our students, and we have standards and expectations.

42. Walk Gently

It's easy to become caught up in the frenetic pace of demanding routines, rushing from one class to another and from one day to the next. When this happens, you can lose track of not only yourself and your own well-being, but also of what's important.

Slowing down takes mindfulness. It means breaking habits and rhythms that have become patterned and ingrained. However, it is worth becoming more aware of what is going on around us and more aware of how we are in the world.

The result can be to clear the mind and to appreciate that not everything has to be rushed. This in turn can give us a greater appreciation for what we do and how we do it. It helps us to understand both ourselves and others.

Time, we know, shares many of the same verbs as money, at least in English. We save time, we don't waste time, we spend time, we earn time, we need time, we want time. These are all purposeful verbs with specific connotations of value or desire.

Taking time, however, is different. To take time, in a positive sense, means to be deliberative and purposeful. It also connotes being able to enjoy the process you are passing through in time. It is a reflective state.

43. Move Right

I like to think of teaching as performance. Effective teaching requires the teacher to captivate the audience. How we move says a lot about who we are and how we feel, not only about ourselves but our students and our classroom. How we stand, how we move about the classroom, how we display the board or block it, how we signal to students --- these actions all need to be clear and deliberate. Even in a student-centered class, the teacher is still the facilitator and director, the source of knowledge and authority. The way we move reflects our level of interest and our conviction in what we do.

One way to think about this is to imagine you are on stage and that your students are your audience. Everyone needs to be able to see you and to hear you. Students also need to be able to see the board and be clear about what you are doing. Moving deliberately and with authority helps give you a sense of presence, of being in control; this in turn helps the students focus. There is a certain amount of stagecraft in teaching. Watch yourself move in a mirror or video yourself. It can be fun to see how you move and also to work on aspects of your movements, such as how you stand or walk across the classroom.

Movement is something we can all work on. Not only do we need to move right, we need to move period. The teacher needs to circulate, to address all students, to move around the classroom and be present for all students.

Enter the classroom with conviction and leave with confidence. The way we move should reflect that we are confident, organized, committed, and professional. Not only do we want to give clear positive messages about ourselves, we can subliminally model positive behaviors for students.

Yourself

44. Find Your Inner Teacher

Everyone has an image of what a teacher should be like and their own image of how they would like to be as a teacher. This is an outward view and a good place to begin, but the real work of honing one's teaching self involves finding one's inner teacher.

Our inner teacher is the one who is true to ourselves and our dispositions. It is not someone else. It is you, complete with your strengths and weaknesses. A teacher who is struggling to be someone else or not accepting of who they are will exhaust themselves and find it difficult to grow both individually and professionally.

To find your inner teacher, you need to reflect on why you do things the way you do and what your comfort zone is. Reflect on your fears and anxieties and areas for growth.

Reflection can be done in terms of journaling; that is, keeping a record not only of what you did but also of how you felt, and how your students reacted and how you think they felt. It's important to be honest and to acknowledge how you actually felt. If you were angry or upset, write it down.

Reflection can also be done with a peer – perhaps someone you work with and can talk to, or someone you interact with on social media. This needs to be someone you trust and respect, and someone who is also interested in growing and developing as a teacher. Reflection involves confronting one's fears and anxieties. At first this might seem daunting, but over time it becomes empowering, as you begin to realize that you can overcome anything.

Your inner teacher is authentic. You have to feel like 'you' when you teach; in fact, you must *be* you when you teach. We can borrow techniques and ideas from other teachers, but we must make them ours and use them in a way that works for us.

Students notice the teacher who is authentic and is true to their own inner teacher.

45. Forgive Yourself

Teaching is a difficult art to master. It takes time, practice, and reflection to become the teacher you must ultimately feel comfortable with – yourself. It also requires inner growth and the development of skills to help you differentiate between the practice of teaching and the emotions you feel as a teacher.

For example, it is natural to think that if an activity or lesson doesn't work, it is either your fault or the students' fault. Or, if a student doesn't listen, one might think, "Why won't you listen to me?" rather than "What's stopping you from listening?" We need to move away from the personal to the procedural. We should examine the instruction and how it was given or the activity or lesson, rather than the 'I' that feels responsible, guilty, or hurt when something doesn't go according to plan.

Forgiving yourself means accepting yourself – which in turn means knowing that you are enough. As you are. That is not to say that you can't improve and acquire a broader skill set, and so become more efficient at what you do, but to expect yourself to be able to do this from the get-go is unreasonable.

Remember that 'perfection' is not a goal. We can always do better, but there is a point where the desire for perfection takes too much time and emotional energy. In this sense, forgiving yourself involves a degree of letting go.

46. Get Comfortable with Being Uncomfortable

This is an important mantra and also an important aspect of being a reflective and dynamic teacher.

Remaining within the comfort or safety zone is limiting. Students like variety and challenge. They don't want to always be doing the same type of activities in the same way. Students are curious and creative, and we need to sate these hungers. To do so, we must try new activities and new techniques. This is risk-taking and it can be uncomfortable, but it's a necessary condition for our professional growth.

We may find that the new activities and techniques we try don't work the first time. That is to be expected, and the solution is simply to reflect, critique, and think of a different way of doing it next time in order to be successful.

The more we take risks, the easier it becomes. We don't need to apologize for failure if it occurs or make excuses. We simply need to be responsive, reflective, and procedural.

47. Get Comfortable with Yourself

You are enough as you are.

Accept that.

We all have attributes and skills, and we all have aspects of ourselves we could work on and improve. We also have skillsets and areas of knowledge that can be expanded and refined. We are an ongoing process.

We are constantly interacting with other and with ourselves. We have an aura and an energy that impacts our moods and every situation we are in. For this reason, we need to accept who we are and get comfortable being unique individuals. There is no need to try to be like someone else – or worse, be someone we are not.

We need to get comfortable with ourselves in order to move more easily through our lives. Teachers who are comfortable with themselves will find it easier to interact with students in a positive and accepting way. The students will be put at ease and feel more relaxed. Their affective filters will lower, and it will be easier for them to engage.

Getting comfortable with yourself is a journey. It takes time and reflection. Again, this is an area where journaling can help. Write a list of skills you feel you have and areas in which you would like to develop and grow. Realize that you are a work in progress. In this way, you bring vulnerabilities to the table and can then begin the process of working on them.

48. Step Outside Yourself

Teaching leads to the development of patterns and routines. This is natural, but can result in 'non-seeing' as we become overly absorbed with our daily concerns.

Stepping outside ourselves allows us to see things in a clearer light. This enables us to critique ourselves, and also means we don't have to use up energy being consumed by anxieties. This, in turn, leaves us with more energy to carry out and reflect on our mission – to teach effectively and efficiently.

Beginning teachers may find it hard to step outside themselves while in the act of teaching. To begin with, then, try to step outside both before and after teaching, in a reflective and critical manner. One technique is to simply have a question framework of 'high yield' questions.

High yield questions are ones that get at underlying motives and fears. For example, "Why is it that I always only follow one particular procedure in class? Is it that I am afraid of changing how I do what I do, even when there may be more effective ways?"

More experienced teachers will become more confident in self-critiquing and develop skills for changing plans in mid-class should the need arise, rather than soldiering blindly on at the risk of emotional stress for the teacher and boredom or frustration for the students.

49. Remember You Are a Teacher

Sometimes we teachers can be so busy with classes and other responsibilities that we are swept up in a frenetic whirl and forget that we are teachers – we simply become busy people in a rush.

At times like these, we need to step back and remember that being a teacher is very important. We are part of the long history of education and play a significant role in the development of human society. This is something to be proud of. It also means we need to be respected and taken seriously. We are professionals. You've probably heard the saying: Those who can, do; and those who can't, teach. It's always bothered me. I would like to say that Those who can, do because of the teachers they had.

However, teaching is also a responsibility that we must take time to reflect on in order to serve not only our students, but ourselves. This, to my mind, is one of the gifts of teaching. Teaching is both a skill and an art, and we can be constantly tweaking and improving our abilities. Remember you are a teacher. Remember that you have committed yourself to a path of growth, and one that will benefit both your students and yourself.

50. Be Wise

This is a simple though complex exhortation. Wisdom means *The quality of having experience, knowledge, and good judgment; the quality of being wise.* To be wise means *To have experience, knowledge, and good judgment.* This is a wonderful quality to have and one that all teachers should aspire to.

New teachers need experience to gain wisdom. This takes time and effort. Through experience, we learn who we are and who our learners are. If we are open to experience and positive in our approach, experience becomes our teacher. By approaching our experience honestly and reflectively, we can become better at teaching and continue to hone our craft. At the same time we garner our experience, we can increase our knowledge and be open to change. The best teachers have many different qualities, but they are all avid learners.

And so, as we increase our experience and expand our knowledge, our judgment will become more refined. As a result, we will make appropriate decisions for our classrooms and our learners, and become the efficient and effective teachers we all aspire to be.

Bonus technique!

51. Remember You Make a Difference

It's important to be proud to be a teacher. It's also important to remember that we make a difference in our students' lives. We may not see the differences we make on a daily basis, but it's worth remembering that we constantly encourage, inspire, model, lead, build, and realize student potential. All of these things make a difference. This, really, is the reason we teach: to make a difference.

(To see an inspiring video on this topic, look for the video on YouTube of poet Taylor Mali's performance of "What Teachers Make.")

And here it's important to remember that it's not what we teach, whether that's English to speakers of other languages or another subject, it's how we teach. The difference we make depends on the supporting, caring, inspiring classroom we create and the community we build. It's through this and the development of trust that we can help students realize their goals and achieve their dreams. This is how we make a difference. And, when all is said and done, there is nothing more satisfying than to see a student succeed.

About the Series

Teaching English as a second or foreign language is full of challenges: How do you hold students' interest? How do you ensure that they get enough practice to really learn? The *Fifty Ways to Teach* series gives you a variety of drills, games, techniques, methods, and ideas to help your students master English. Most of the ideas can be used for both beginning and advanced classes. Many require little to no preparation or special materials. The ideas can be used with any textbook, or without a textbook at all. These short, practical guides aim to make your teaching life easier, and your students' lives more rewarding and successful.

If you have comments or suggestions (such as ideas for future books that you would find useful), feel free to contact the publisher at editor@wayzgoosepress. com, check out the offerings on our publishing website at http://wayzgoosepress.com, or join us on Facebook: facebook.com/WayzgoosePress.

* * *

If your students are motivated, or if they need further practice, consider recommending our titles for students, *Fifty Ways to Practice...* Current titles include Reading, Writing, Grammar, Speaking, and Vocabulary.